PERSONAL
TURNAROUND

JOE JOE DAWSON

ISBN: 978-1-7350800-0-0

Table of Contents

INTRODUCTION

I believe that it is God's desire to get His people ready for what He wants to do in the earth. The church, America and the nations of the earth need a turnaround. But first, God must do a turnaround in our lives personally.

In life and in ministry, I encounter so many people who have an immeasurable amount of potential to do great things with their lives and for God. However, unfortunately, many people never reach their full potential because they need a personal turnaround! Here is the hard truth, my friends, you are the way you are because you are the way you are. But the good news is that God can take anyone or anything and turn it all around!

People often ask me, "Joe Joe, what do you do for a living?" My answer is always the same, "I help move people forward." My hope is that after you read this book you will walk away with 13keys to personal turnaround. I truly believe that if we would each take these keys and use them in our lives, there is no limit to what we could do. There is no limit to God, so there should be no limit to you. God has a breathtaking calling for our lives, but it is our responsibility to steward every talent, ability, and opportunity He has given us.

Often, we look at our lives and want to blame others, our past experiences or failures and say, "If only this or that would have been different then I could have done this or that." This is the wrong mindset! Excuses will keep you stuck in the same spot for years. It is time to lose all the excuses and have a personal turnaround! If you will take these keys and activate them in your life, you will live a life full of purpose and destiny. Personal turnaround is possible and I want to help you get there!

CHAPTER 1
🔥 PRAYER

If you know me, you know that I will find any excuse to go to or host a prayer meeting. I love prayer! When I was younger and first starting out in ministry, I was praying in the sanctuary of the church where I was on staff at that time. As I was seeking the Lord, I asked Him to give me a life verse. I wanted a verse that I could use to help define and shape my life. The Lord immediately spoke to me so clearly, "Mark 1:35." Off the top of my head, I didn't know what Mark 1:35 said. So, I opened my Bible and read, "Now in the morning, having risen a long while before daylight, He went out and departed to a solitary place; and there He prayed." This verse has marked me and the rest of my life since.

Jesus got up very early each morning and found a place where He could spend time with the Father. If Jesus did this, then we need to do the same thing! Jesus understood the power of prayer before the day got started. Jesus Christ, the Chief Apostle of the Church, knew that He would have His disciples and others pulling on His wisdom and time. This is why Jesus knew that He needed to start His day with the foundation of prayer. Numerous times throughout the Scripture, we see Jesus staying up late at night or getting up really early in the morning to spend time with His Father. Our relationship with God, through prayer, is the foundation of everything we do. We have to maintain a fresh, current relationship with the Lord at all times!

The first key is to turnaround your prayer life. If we are looking for a personal turnaround or a breakthrough, then each morning we should be spending time with God. I have heard many people say, "If you own your morning, you own your day." But I want to propose that if God owns your morning, God will own your day! If all of your mornings look like hitting the snooze button over and over, rushing to get yourself and your family ready for the day and running out of the door, you will not experience personal turnaround. Your time of prayer in the morning will set you up for a successful day, and if you will do it consistently, then you will have a successful life. Personal revival and breakthrough happens first in the place of prayer.

Leonard Ravenhill says, "No man is greater than his prayer life." You are no greater than your prayer life. So, how great is your prayer life? Those that I run closely with, I can tell if they have been spending time in the secret place with God or not. Everything that has ever been built that has lasting value has been given to people in the place of prayer. If whatever you are putting your hands to was birthed in the place of prayer, then it will stand. Those that have built their lives around the presence of God and the power of prayer can withstand the tests of time, critics and attacks of the enemy. We become strong and steadfast when we are people of prayer.

Matthew 6:6 says, "But you, when you pray, go into your room, and when you have shut your door, pray to your Father who is in the secret place; and your Father who sees in secret will reward you openly." We see the words "you" or "your" eight times in this verse. This tells us that we have to take responsibility to get ourselves into a quiet spot, shut the door, and get alone with God. When we are consistent in private prayer, God will always show up in a mighty and powerful way. God rewards those who diligently seek Him and He does so openly. When we get into the secret place with God, He reveals His heart to us and teaches us how to pray. Then, we are rewarded to see what we pray for coming to pass openly. This is where any personal turnaround begins!

Matthew 6:33 says, "But seek first the Kingdom of God and His righteousness, and all these things shall be added unto you." This scripture teaches us that the first thing we should seek is the Kingdom of God. Many people go to prayer with a long list of things that they need God to do for them. The first thing you need to do is seek the face of Father God. When you go into the place of prayer, pray for the Kingdom of God to come to earth! Seek the Kingdom first because when you take care of Father God's business, He will take care of yours. Many times, we may get so caught up praying the heart of God that we forget to even pray for our own personal needs. But that's ok! The Lord does not just hear our needs; He also fulfills them for us.

Many people are unstable in their mind and their emotions because they have not made prayer the foundation of their walk with God. Time spent in prayer brings stability and wisdom because in prayer we hear from God. He can lead and direct us perfectly if we position ourselves to hear from Him. Samuel Chadwick says, "The man who prays is irresistible to God. That is why the devil puts so many obstacles in his way." If you are a person of prayer, you are irresistible to God and the enemy will try to fight you. However, do not be discouraged! Whatever obstacles or attacks come your way, God will come through on your behalf. In Daniel 5:27, the three Hebrew boys came out of the fiery furnace unharmed and not even smelling like smoke! God protects and defends people of prayer.

Proverbs 8:17 says, "I love those who love me, and those who seek me diligently find me." In my opinion, diligently seeking the Lord looks like rising up early in the morning or staying up late at night to pray. However, it doesn't matter when you set time aside to spend time in prayer. It is just important that you do. Find a time that you can set aside every day to devote to God. In my own life, I try to schedule three times a day that I spend time in prayer.

Making prayer a part of your day-to-day life will help you accomplish your daily assignment from God, which over time means you will reach your destiny. When you seek God diligently, you will experience personal turnaround. Prayer changes everything!

CHAPTER 2
DECLARATIONS & DECREES

Many people in the church either do not believe in declarations and decrees or are unsure about them. I was once having a conversation with a man who had been in church his entire life. After hearing one of my messages, he said, "I'm not sure about those declarations and decrees." I asked him, "What kind of Bible do you read, sir?" He proudly answered, "King James Version." I told him, "Did you know the word "decree" is in the King James Version 55 times and declaration is used 4 times?" He answered, "Well, I've never read it." I politely said, "Well, you must not have read the whole thing!"

Declarations and decrees can change everything. They are important because they are part of the authority God has given us. Think about it, how was the world formed? Through a declaration! God made a declaration and whatever He spoke, it came into being. This is why making a declaration or a decree is a key factor in seeing a personal turnaround. When we speak, creative power is released. Declarations and decrees can change situations and circumstances. They can change your mind, your life and you!

So, what is a declaration? A declaration is a formal announcement of a being or of a state or condition. There will be times in your life that you need to make a formal announcement about your life and who you are in God. You will need to make a declaration about yourself. Personal declarations are powerful for personal turnaround. Every morning I make declarations over myself. I make declarations about my spiritual life, my physical health, my finances and over my family.

Several years ago, my daughter Malachi was laughing at me one morning as I made a declaration about that day being a great and beautiful day. Malachi said, "Dad, it is August in Texas. It is 100 degrees outside and you just said it's a beautiful day! You say that when it's freezing cold in the winter and when it's pouring rain in the spring. You say that every day." I replied, "Every day is a great day. It doesn't matter to me what the weather is like outside because my mindset is that every day is a great day!" All the days of my life I want to make positive declarations, formal announcements about my life and over the people God has placed in my life. You must make up your mind to make declarations over yourself.

A decree is a declaration made by a legal authority. This is powerful because you have been made a legal authority by Heaven. The Bible says that we are joint-heirs with Jesus Christ. Where is Jesus Christ right now? He is at the right hand of the Father seated in Heavenly places. Since we are joint-heirs with Jesus, we are also seated in Heavenly places with Him. You have authority, so make decrees! This is why we must make decrees because we have authority.

We never fight for victory, we only fight from victory. From the beginning of the foundation of the world, God destined you to be His reflection in the earth, ruling and reigning over the enemy with His authority! Hosea 4:6 says, "My people are destroyed for the lack of knowledge." If we really knew how powerful declarations and decrees can be, we would constantly be making declarations and decrees.

As we journey through life, it is easy to grow stagnant within the normality of life. This is why we must make it a habit to declare and decree the will of God. It's easy to get caught in the rhythm of the day to day and settle into that. But what we must realize is what God is doing in the earth right now. God is moving, shaking and stirring many people in this hour. We must partner with Heaven by decreeing and declaring for the Kingdom of God to be manifested in the earth as it is in Heaven.

Luke 10:19 says, "Behold, I give you the authority to trample on serpents and scorpions, and over all the power of the enemy, and nothing shall by any means hurt you." What has Jesus given us power and authority over? Everything! This is why when we make a declaration or a decree it will come to pass! The enemy has no power over you. You are a legal authority in the spiritual realm because of your relationship with God. You don't have to tolerate anything the enemy tries to throw your way. Stand up and fight! Make declarations and decrees and watch as things begin to change and shift in your life.

In Job 13:17 God says to Job, "Keep listening to my words, and let my declaration be in your ears." God spoke to Job in the midst of his trials to encourage Job to stand up and fight by declaring and decreeing the will of God for his life. God was making this declaration over Job to stop his complaining and shift him into declaring what God truly intended for his life.

1 Peter 2:9 says, "But you are a chosen generation, a royal priesthood, a holy nation, His own special people, that you may proclaim the praises of Him who called you out of darkness into His marvelous light." This is a powerful truth

from the word of God. The Word declares that you are a royal priesthood and a holy nation. If God declares this over you, you need to declare this over yourself.

The truth is, many people do not have a personal turnaround because they have never declared their personal turnaround. Many have promises from God that they never declared or decreed. If you haven't seen it come to pass you need to decree for it to be manifested in your life. Even if your mind cannot see it and your heart cannot feel it you need to decree it out of your mouth. You need to trust the prophetic words and promises that God has spoken over your life enough to speak them over yourself! The more you declare and decree the promises of God over your life the more they will be manifested in your life. Get your personal turnaround by declaring and decreeing your personal turnaround!

CHAPTER 3
🔥 FASTING

Our next key for personal turnaround is not the most popular, but it is very powerful. In this chapter, we will talk about fasting as a key for personal turnaround. Fasting is one of the most powerful weapons we have in the Spirit, but it is one of the most unused as well. Many believers do not fast because they are not serious about what they are believing God to do. Furthermore, there are many believers who have been in church their entire lives but have never heard a single sermon on fasting! The church at large does not teach fasting because very few people fast. Fasting kills the flesh. Fasting humbles and properly aligns us with the Lord. Fasting is a powerful key that can unlock personal and corporate breakthroughs, turnaround, and freedom.

Fasting is mentioned throughout the entire Bible. The Word of God tells us that, after He was baptized, the Holy Spirit drove Jesus into the wilderness to fast for 40 days. This was the first thing Jesus did after being baptized! He had been officially released by the Father for public ministry and, instead of beginning to minister to the crowds, Jesus immediately went on a fast. He knew the power of fasting. If fasting was important to Jesus, it should be that much more important to us!

Several years ago, my wife and I went through a very difficult season. A major transition came into our life and ministry that we were blindsided by and we responded through fasting and prayer. That year I fasted over 100 days because I was desperate to hear from God and wasn't fully relying on God to breakthrough for us. The amount of breakthrough and deliverance I experienced during that season of fasting was astronomical. During that season of intense fasting, I learned that fasting needed to become a regular part of my lifestyle. I learned to not wait until I needed a breakthrough to fast. I wanted to become a person who lived a lifestyle of fasting because fasting does not change God, it changes you. Your mindset and your perspective are shifted by fasting. Whenever I become frustrated with a situation or an individual I will fast and pray. Then God reveals His heart and His perspective about whatever is going on. Unfortunately, many of us only fast when we are completely desperate. However, if you can learn to make fasting a part of your lifestyle you will see personal turnaround in your life!

On a practical note, you may want to make fasting a part of your schedule. You may want to choose one day of the week that you fast every week. You may want to choose a specific month that you do a particular fast each year. Whatever it looks like for you, make fasting a habit in your life and you will live a fasted lifestyle. We often fast for spiritual reasons, as we should, but fasting also has natural benefits. Dr. Myles Monroe said, "Fasting is God's reset button for the body." I have often found that toward the end of a period of fasting, I will have more energy and feel better physically than when I am not fasting. Your natural body responds to fasting by flushing out toxins and giving your digestive system a much-needed rest. When God introduced the spiritual discipline of fasting, He knew that it would benefit us physically as well as spiritually.

Whenever you fast, it is crucial that you also set time apart to pray. Take the time that you would spend eating and preparing food and spend that time in prayer. Fasting without prayer has little power. It is the combination of prayer and fasting that draws us to the Lord and invites Heaven to move on our behalf. If you are fasting without prayer, you are just on a diet! If my wife and I are both fasting, we will of course still make meals for our children. We will sit down with our children and spend time with them while they are eating. Even during a fast, we do not neglect to spend time with our family. Sometimes, we will even take turns sitting with our kids during meals so that the other can spend time in prayer.

Fasting should draw us to desire more of God and stir up spiritual hunger in us. So, don't fast without prayer!

When you fast, you will experience more of the power of God. Fasting unlocks miracles and breakthrough. Sometimes we fast for personal reasons, other times we fast for corporate breakthrough and other times we fast to intercede for others, for our nation or government or for something specific God lays on our hearts. Fasting must become a regular part of your life. Before you finish a fast, go ahead and plan your next fast. It is easy to fall out of a fasted lifestyle but, if you will be intentional, you will see fasting change everything.

In Matthew 6:16, Jesus says, "When you fast..." Take note that He said, "When you fast," not, "If you fast." This means that as followers of Jesus we should fast. Whenever I hear someone say, "Well, I don't know if fasting is necessary. I don't know if it is for me." I immediately think of this scripture. Jesus looked at His disciples and said to them, "When you fast..." This means that

He had an expectation that His followers and disciples would fast! Matthew 6:16 says, "When you fast, don't be sad-faced like the hypocrites. For they make their faces unattractive so their fasting is obvious to people. I assure you: They've got their reward!" Jesus is warning His disciples to try not to look spiritual or make their fasting obvious. However, He was challenging them to fast and to fast often. If you are a child of God, you are called to fast because fasting breaks cycles, strongholds, wrong mindsets, and bondage. If you are serious about breaking out of a cycle, go on a fast! One of the names for the devil is Beelzebub which means Lord of the flies. The life cycle of a fly is 40 days! This is why we see so many examples of 40-day fasts in scripture because 40 days can break any cycle of the enemy.

In one season of my life, I felt led to go on a 40-day Daniel Fast. Towards the end of the fast, I wanted to extend the fast! I kept praying and asking the Lord if I could extend it out to 45 days. However, I felt the Lord say no. A week after being off of the fast, I felt the release to go on another 40-day Daniel Fast. After I completed the second 40 day Fast, I couldn't even drink sweet tea anymore. I am from the South and used to absolutely love sweet tea! However, during my time of fasting, my appetite changed. Fasting changes our physical appetite. Our spiritual appetite also changes and we begin to crave the presence and things of God more than anything else. Fasting will change you spiritually, but it will also break unhealthy natural habits.

In Matthew 17, we see that the disciples of Jesus were trying to cast out a demon from a little boy that kept having seizures. The little boy would throw himself into fire and water but the disciples were not able to set him free. Jesus healed and delivered the little boy with ease, but His disciples were frustrated. The disciples had used the same words Jesus used and had been given authority when He sent them out, so they asked Jesus why they could not cast out the demon from the boy. Jesus replied in Matthew 17:21, "This kind does not go out except by prayer and fasting." Fasting breaks strongholds and releases the power of God to destroy demonic bondage. The disciples were looking for the power to come from the right words or even just from the authority that Jesus had given to them. However, the power needed to see the boy delivered could only come through prayer and fasting.

Your greatest breakthrough is often on the other side of your obedience to fast. Miracles are manifested when we fast. Prayers we have prayed for years are suddenly answered when we seek God in prayer and fasting. Again, fasting is one of the most powerful spiritual weapons we have been given. Don't let it go unused in your life. Fasting is a vital key for personal turnaround!

CHAPTER 4
ⓤ SOWING

Hosea 4:6 tells us that people are destroyed because of a lack of knowledge. This truth grips me because I do not want to see anyone fail or get derailed because they do not know any better. Many people suffer and struggle because there are certain Biblical principles that they just don't know about or do not understand. One of the biggest areas I see people destroyed because of a lack of knowledge is in the area of finances.

If we read in the Gospels about the topics Jesus spoke about, money is one of the things Jesus talked about the most. Throughout scripture, the Bible addresses the subject of money and giving more times than most people realize. For whatever reason, money is a very touchy subject. So, people often do not talk about it, especially in the Church. However, Jesus did not mind bringing up money and finances and neither do I! I don't mind talking about money and Kingdom finances because if we can be good stewards of the financial seed God entrusts to us, then we can succeed!

I want to talk to you about how Kingdom finances, sowing and being wise stewards of money can be a strategic part of personal turnaround. One of the things my wife and I do each year is to try to give more than the year before. Several years ago, we had a record year of giving. We gave to our church, to our apostle, to different ministries we glean from and we were proud of that. We love to give and sow finances into the Kingdom of God. We give because we want to and because we love God. However, we also give because, throughout scripture, we have seen how obedience in giving and generosity opens up God's blessings in the lives of believers.

Matthew 6:33 says, "But seek first the Kingdom of God and His righteousness, and all these things shall be added to you." Think about this verse within the context of giving. Whenever income comes into our hands, the first thing my wife and I do is to give. We don't look at bills or things we want or need. We give first. I minister to and speak with many different people who call me asking for prayer or advice because they are having financial issues. One of the first things I always ask them is, "Are you giving tithes and offering?" Many times, their answer is, "No." I often tell people, "If you are not tithing or giving, you cannot expect to be free from financial problems." Malachi 3:8-10 tells us that if we do not give our tithe, then we are cursed with a curse! I would much rather have 90% of my finances and be blessed than have 100% of my finances and be cursed.

Many people argue over whether the tithe is still required because it is an "Old Testament" principle. I don't waste my time arguing theological stances about giving. My desire is to give because I trust God but also because

I believe His promises concerning giving can be trusted. I do not limit my giving to only the tithe. Autumn and I choose to give tithes and offerings. Our goal is to give much more than 10% to God because we are givers and believe in Kingdom finances.

If money cannot hold you, then money cannot hold you. When you are pursuing what God has called you to do, you cannot allow yourself to try to figure out how you will take care of it financially in the natural. If you allow yourself to worry about how you will pay for the vision God has given you, then you will never step out and act on it. Matthew 6:22 says, "The lamp of the body is the eye. If therefore your eye is single, your whole body will be full of light." If you focus on the Kingdom of God in everything and you are singularly focused, everything will work out.

2 Corinthians 9:6 says, "...He who sows sparingly will also reap sparingly, and he who sows bountifully will also reap bountifully." Ask yourself this question, "Am I reaping sparingly?" If the answer is yes, then you may be sowing

sparingly. God wants to see you prosper but you must sow seed to reap a harvest. I believe in miracles and breakthrough as much as anyone. However, the truth is that if we do not heed the principle of sowing and reaping God Himself established, we cannot expect to receive a harvest. Imagine if a farmer never planted any seed in his field. Imagine if he went out into his field at harvest time and started kicking the ground and complaining because there were no crops or fruit. Everyone knows that would be ridiculous, but I encounter so many people who treat their giving and finances this way. They never give or sow into the Kingdom of God but expect God to bless them financially. It does not work that way, my friends! The good news is that God honors the principle of sowing and reaping. Galatians 6:7 says, "Do not be deceived, God is not mocked; for whatever a man sows, that he will also reap."

People who prosper in life are givers. Luke 6:38 says, "Give, and it will be given to you: good measure, pressed down, shaken together, and running over will be put into your bosom. For with the same measure that you use, it will be measured back to you." If you are generous, God will send generous people into your life to return your generosity. I once heard someone say, "You cannot out give God." That is the truth. The ministers that people criticize and speak negatively about the most are those that are prosperous. If you are not a generous or prosperous person, you will be critical of those who are. God is always looking for ways to bless you. In order to receive those blessings, we must be obedient to all of His principles and that includes in our finances.

Mark 4:20 tells us that when we sow, some will reap thirtyfold, some sixty, and some a hundredfold. You will reap more than what you sow every single time. There is so much power in one seed. One apple seed can produce over 12,000 apples and 144,000 seeds. You don't know what your one seed of $10, $50, $100 or $1,000 can do. Be willing to sow whatever God has placed in your hand. He will multiply whatever you sow.

I want to share this piece of wisdom with you, your job is not the source of your money. Your job is your resource and God is your source. Many people become frantic whenever they lose or step out of a job because they believe their job is their source. Wherever your streams of income come from are the resource and God is the source. When one stream of income stops, don't panic. Remember that God is your source. God will do whatever He needs to do in order to provide for you. It is our responsibility to stay connected to the source, to sow and be good stewards of everything God places in our hands. God will take care of the rest.

CHAPTER 5
🔥 APPLICATION

In life and in ministry, I encounter and interact with many different types of people from all different places and lifestyles. As I've encountered so many people, I have realized that many of them never reach their full potential because they do not have a good work ethic. You may be thinking, "Well that doesn't sound very spiritual." However, the truth is many have an amazing relationship with God and have good intentions but never do anything with their lives because they are unwilling to work.

Growing up, my dad was a cattle farmer. He instilled in me at a very young age a strong work ethic that I've carried into everything I do.

When I was just a kid, my dad bought me a dairy cow and two little calves. He told me that it was my full responsibility to take care of them and if anything happened to them he would make me carry them off and bury them! I learned very early that working hard and succeeding go hand in hand. In order to reach your full potential in life, you must have a strong work ethic.

I've seen so many gifted and talented individuals who remain unsuccessful because they do not know how to apply what God has given them. Application is the work it takes to see what God has given you and what He has promised come to pass. When we learn the proper application we will step into personal turnaround and whatever we put our hands to will succeed.

Habakkuk 2:2-3 says, "Write the vision and make it plain on tablets, that he may run who reads it. For the vision is yet for an appointed time; But at the end it will speak, and it will not lie. Though it tarries, wait for it; because it will surely come, it will not tarry." This is what we must understand. As soon as God gives you a vision or a dream, the devil will immediately come and try to steal your vision. The enemy may try to talk you out of it by bringing doubt and unbelief. He may try to make you feel unworthy or ill-equipped to carry it out. Whatever he does, the devil wants to steal the vision God has given you so that it will always just be a vision and never become a reality. This is why it is so important that we apply the instructions of Habakkuk 2:2. Get the vision God has for your life, write it down and run with it! Don't stop to question it, don't stop to listen to the enemy. Just run with the vision and apply it!

My wife, Autumn has a vision board hanging up right next to the sink she uses in our bathroom. I know exactly what the vision God has given to my wife looks like because she has made it plain and put it on her vision board. Every day you need to look at the vision God has given you and go over it with the Lord. Pray over it, declare and decree for it to come to pass and apply it in your life! This is how I pray every single day over the vision God has given me, "Holy Spirit, put Your dreams in my heart. When I move, act, and go about my day I'm applying what You have put in my heart to do."

Every day of my life I fast and pray like it all depends on God and I work like it all depends on me. Why? Because it does! The world is outdoing the body of Christ because the world knows how to apply and work for what they think they are supposed to do. It is a delicate balance as a Christian. We must depend on God and stay in the place of prayer. However, we must also learn to apply and work toward whatever God has called us to accomplish. When I first started traveling to minister, I connected with a handful of other ministers who were just starting to travel as well. I am now one of the only ones still traveling and ministering. Why? I believe it is because some of them were working and networking to try to get speaking engagement but forgot the place of prayer. On the other hand, I think some of them got so deep on the prayer side of things that they never worked. To see personal turnaround we must learn to balance both.

I believe many people go around the same mountains and find themselves in the same position over and over again because they simply have not learned how to apply what God has given to them. In order to experience personal turnaround we must learn to apply ourselves and work toward the vision and the dream God has given to us. Prayer and time spent in the presence of God will keep our hearts pure and the vision God has for us fresh in our minds. Work and application will keep you moving forward and not sitting idle. Run with whatever God has called you to do! Run with the vision and the gifts God has placed in your life and saturate it in prayer. Apply it and see the overflow hit everything you put your hands to!

God gives each of us gifts, talents, and abilities to manifest His Kingdom. How many people are waiting for you to do what God has called you to do? If you never work what God has given you how will His Kingdom be advanced? If you never put in any work, how will you ever reap a harvest? Personal turnaround comes when we learn to apply what God has given us.

CHAPTER 6
PROPHETIC PROMISES

God gives us prophetic promises to encourage and give us vision to move forward. A prophetic promise from God is one of the most powerful things you will ever have! A prophetic promise is something you can always fight with, wielding it like a sword in battle against the enemy. However, what you do with your promises and prophetic words will determine whether or not you ever experience personal turnaround.

Why does your spirit leap whenever you receive a prophetic word? Why do you become excited when God gives you a prophetic promise? It is because a fresh word from God hits your spirit and causes it to come alive like nothing else will. Before the foundation of the world was laid God had a plan for your life. When you hear a prophetic word or promise you are getting a glimpse of what God has planned for you. This should be exciting! However, it is not enough to just have a prophetic word or a promise from God. We must steward them wisely or they will not come to pass.

Many times believers will receive a prophetic word, get excited about it but then never do anything with that prophetic promise. Noah had a prophetic word from God to build an arc and promised that if he did God would save him and his entire family. What if Noah just sat around with his prophetic word from God and never built the arc? He would have been swept away in the flood with everyone else! It is important that we put action to whatever God speaks to us.

I want to challenge you with this question, "What are you doing with the word of God that is in your heart and all the prophetic words that have been spoken over you?" James 1:22 says,

"But be doers of the word, and not hearers only, deceiving yourselves." It is important that you record or write down everything that God speaks to you. This is the first step to stewarding your prophetic promises. You cannot steward something you don't remember! Whether it is a prophetic word God speaks to you through someone else or something He speaks straight to you. Make sure you document that prophetic word by writing it down or recording it.

Many people go to church every Sunday, chase down revivals or their favorite speaker and never do anything for the Lord besides attending a service. It is time for the prophetic seeds lying dormant in your life to come alive. Become a doer of the word of God and start living out the prophetic destiny that He has for your life. No longer deceive yourself or try to talk yourself out of the prophetic words that God has given you. When it's all said and done more may be said than done. Let that never be said about you! Instead, be a doer of the word of God. Dr. Myles Munroe said, "You can have what you can manage." Do you want a fresh prophetic word from God? Then manage the last word God gave you. God gives more to those who steward what they already have. Never become satisfied watching somebody else do what they were called to do without fulfilling your own destiny. Ask the Lord today to reveal to you the next step that you need to take toward your prophetic promises.

Unfortunately, so many people will back up at the first sign of resistance. Many receive a prophetic word and start moving towards it only to encounter roadblocks and obstacles. Some become frustrated and worn out in the process before they reach the promise. If you are going to receive your personal turnaround you cannot give up on the prophetic promises God has given you because they are powerful! A prophetic word is like a seed that God plants inside of us. If it is given the chance to grow and stay planted it can grow to be something so powerful. However, the enemy would love nothing more than to steal your prophetic promise when it is still in seed form. When you receive a prophetic promise from God, protect and guard it as if your life depends on it because it does! The enemy will send toxic people into your life to hinder your prophetic seed's growth. You may be running with people who are after your seed. Don't put your seed around people who do not value it. There will always be people who want to steal your seed because they do not have their own harvest. You need to get toxic people out of your life. People who only want to take from you need to be removed from your life. They are only there to try to steal your seed. Proverbs 27:17 says, "Iron sharpens iron and a man sharpens the countenance of his friends." The Bible does not say, one pours out and the other takes all the time. That is called an unbalanced, unhealthy relationship. Any healthy relationship requires both give and take. You must surround yourself with people that do not devalue, hinder or envy your seed. Protecting that prophetic seed is so important in stewarding your prophetic promises.

I believe many people find themselves discouraged or feel stuck simply because they need to reclaim the prophetic words they have laid down. Many have laid down prophetic promises but it is time to reclaim them! How do you reclaim a prophetic promise? Well, first you must remember it. Go back over all of your old prayer journals, prophetic journals, and dream journals. You may have to dig out an old CD or tape that has a prophetic word on it and listen to it again.

If you've given up on a promise from God before you've seen it come to pass it is never too late. As you remember those prophetic promises, ask the Lord to allow you to experience them as if it was the very first time you heard them. Words from God have a transformational way of always remaining fresh and alive.

In order to properly steward your prophetic words, you must declare them until they fully come to pass in your life. Personal turnaround will come when you infuse fresh faith into the prophetic promises God has spoken over your life. We must be found in the place of prayer declaring and decreeing the prophetic words and promises God has given to us. A fresh wind of the Holy Spirit will come to stir up those prophetic promises and God is going to do every single thing He has promised you. But remember, it is our responsibility to reclaim every prophetic word and contend for them to be fully manifested.

It is time for your personal turnaround! You were created for such a time as this to do everything that God placed on your heart to do. Go live out the prophetic promises God has spoken over your life and destiny!

CHAPTER 7
⦿ MENTORS

I truly believe that who you surround and align yourself with is one of the most important keys to success. If you want to experience personal turnaround you need to make sure you are connected to the right people. You also need to make sure you are not connected to the wrong people!

You can accomplish anything in life if you find the right mentor, the right spiritual mother or father to speak into your life. A God-given relationship with a mentor can either make or break you. One of the saddest things I've seen in the body of Christ is people with unlimited potential, who are so gifted and talented, who never reach true success because they did not have a mentor. I've met many people who just never had a mentor or spiritual parent come alongside them to help equip or train them. I've also seen those that had mentors who were willing to come alongside them but because of fear, pride or past negative experiences they refused to be mentored. Don't let this be said of you.

Personal turnaround can be unlocked in your life just by connecting with the right spiritual parent or mentor. I don't care who you are or how much knowledge you may have, you need someone in your life that will always be there to speak into your life. Some of the generals in the faith that I respect the most are in their 60's and 70's and each of them still have mentors! You never outgrow your need to grow, learn and change. Therefore, you will never outgrow your need for a mentor.

Throughout the New Testament, the Apostle Paul wrote letters of instruction and encouragement to the people he spiritually fathered or mentored. The entire book of Timothy was Paul's letter of fatherly advice and instruction for his spiritual son, Timothy. Paul was passionate about seeing those he mentored move forward in their walk with God and in their personal assignments for the Kingdom of God. Mentors are those who are passionate about molding and shaping you into exactly who God has called you to become. A great spiritual father or mother longs to pour into those around them and see them go even further than they ever could. Find a mentor that is passionate about the things of God and wants to see you succeed!

Proverbs 27:17 says, "Iron sharpens iron, so one man sharpens another." Get around sharp people that can help sharpen you! I am a very relational person and believe that personal relationships with spiritual parents and mentors are crucial. However, you can also be mentored by someone without ever meeting them. Some of the people who have mentored me the most are men and women of God who I've never even spent any time with! I find different mentors in resources like books and podcasts. I've been through seasons where I have been drawn to certain ministers or business experts and spent many hours consuming their wisdom and knowledge through the content they create. Find a mentor that resonates with you in your season and glean from and be sharpened by them.

A true mentor is not a counselor! Instead a mentor is someone who is sent into your life to equip, encourage and train you. A great spiritual father or mother will not baby you or allow you to make excuses. They will call out the greatness in you and equip you to move forward in whatever and whoever God has called you to be.

Many people become discouraged when a spiritual child or someone they mentored walks away from them. Don't let this keep you from continuing to pour into those coming behind you! Proverbs 22:6 says, "Train up a child in the way that they should go and when they are old they will not depart from it." This scripture does not only apply to our natural children, it can also apply to our spiritual children as well. A great mentor can see the greatness inside of you before you can. A true spiritual father of mother will see the gold in the midst of the dirt. God uses mentors to call out the potential, gifts, talents, and abilities in others that cannot see it in themselves.

Just like with anything else in life, relationships even with mentors grow and change in different seasons. In the many years of ministry that Autumn and I have been a part of, we have seen numerous people come and go from our lives and leadership. So, we have learned to impart as much as we can to every person knowing not everyone will walk with us forever.

2 Timothy 2:2 says, "And the things that you have heard from me among many witnesses, commit these to faithful men who will be able to teach others also." Paul writes this instructing Timothy to take the things that Paul has demonstrated with his actions and the things he has taught Timothy and instill them into others. He is encouraging Timothy to take what he has learned from Paul and find those that will value it and pour it into them. Whenever you have

received something from a mentor in your life you will pass it down to each person you mentor. This is how legacies are birthed and how they carry on from generation to generation.

In order to see a turnaround in a generation we must first see personal turnaround individually. We glean from mentors and spiritual parents in our own lives and then pass on what we have learned from them to those coming after us. However, I've learned that we must wisely choose who we pour into. Proverbs 9:9 says, "Give instruction to a wise man, and he will be still wiser; Teach a just man, and he will increase in learning." I've been asked before, "Why are you so selective with who you disciple?" I've given many answers but it comes down to this; I cannot afford to waste my time pouring into someone who does not want to learn, change or grow. To help someone move forward in anything they must want to move forward themselves. I only want to cook for someone who is hungry. I only want to pour into someone who is passionate about the things of God. I only want to spend time disciplining someone who is willing to die to the flesh and go after their God-given purpose and destiny.

Many fail because they do not have someone speaking into their life. Proverbs 15:22 says, "Without consultation, plans are frustrated, but with many counselors they succeed." You must have wise mentors and spiritual counsel in your life. Listen to those God has sent into your life and you will succeed. Reach your full potential, fulfill your destiny, and experience personal turnaround by finding the right men and women of God to mentor you!

CHAPTER 8
ⓤ GIFTS

In one translation Proverbs 18:16 says, "Would you like to meet a very important person? Take a generous gift. It will do wonders to gain entrance into His presence." In another translation Proverbs 18:16 says, "A man's gift makes room for him and brings him before great people." When someone who is gifted uses their gifting and becomes successful there will always be those who criticize and oppose them.

Every single person has God-given gifts, talents, and abilities. Steve Harvey defines as a gift as, "The thing you do the best with the least amount of effort." What is that in your life? What gifts and talents God has given you? Whatever they are, apply them and work them. Put your hands to what God has gifted you and graced you to do and watch your life explode! When you find your gift you will never want to stop. Proverbs 18:16 says, "A man's gift makes room for him, and brings him before great men." When you step into your gift, doors will begin to open for you that you never even dreamed of!

The Word of God says that your gift will make room for you. If I am in a service and I sense that we need to pray to open up the atmosphere, I will always look around the room and find someone with a strong prayer life and a gift of intercession. If I sense that God wants to release something prophetic I will ask my wife, who is a prophet, to come up and prophesy. Different gifts are needed in different moments. Not just in services or conferences but in the workplace, the grocery store and in families! God sent you to the earth with a gift not so you could bury it and never use it. No! He gave you the gifts and talents you have to advance the Kingdom of God and for it to bless others and you!

Have you ever thought about how unique you are? I'm talking about your individual giftings, talents and abilities that God gave you. The reason that God gave you all of these specific abilities is for His purpose.

So many people make a living off of their God-given talents but do they ever make an impact for the Kingdom of God with their gifts? 1 Timothy 4:14-15 says, "Do not neglect the gift that is in you, which was given to you by prophecy with the laying on of the hands of the eldership. Meditate on these things; give yourself entirely to them, that your progress may be evident to all."

God has given you every talent and ability that you need to accomplish your destiny. He has gifted you for your purpose and for His purpose. The Lord gave the body of Christ the five-fold giftings of apostles, prophets, pastors, evangelists and teachers in order to equip the church. Who will go unequipped if you keep the gift God has given you dormant inside of you? God's desire is to see you rise up and use the gifting He has given you not just for yourself but also for others.

When you are running on all cylinders, operating fully in the gifting God has placed on your life, it will declare the greatness of God to everyone you come in contact with. People will see the process that you went through to get to the promise and every person who knows you will see the evidence of God's hand upon you. Seeing you walk in your gifting will encourage them to give their lives wholeheartedly to the purpose that God has placed on their own life.

God has uniquely gifted every single one of us and never, not even for one moment, think that God has forgotten about you. He has not misplaced you. He is simply waiting for you to overcome your fear and insecurity and step into the call He has on your life. The Holy Spirit is guiding you through life, which may seem like an obstacle course at sometimes, but you're going to make it through just fine. Proverbs 19:21 says, "Many are the plans in a person's heart, but it is the Lord's purpose that prevails." The Lord has an amazing way of always making His purpose come to pass. Sometimes it even seems when we have messed things up or circumstances have messed things, all mighty powerful God still has a way of getting us to where He needs us to be. The Word of God says, "The giftings are calling of God are irrevocable." Another translation says, "they are under full warranty." It is never too late and you are never too far gone for God to restore you and use you in your gifting. God has not given up on your destiny so neither should you!

Before, we were ever even formed in our mother's womb, we were created in the heart and mind of God. God, the good Father has placed a mighty, purposeful, powerful gifting inside each of us. This is why the gift mix that God has given you will sustain you and help move you forward into the destiny God has for you. No one is born worthless. Hard situations, circumstances, trials, tests and things people or the enemy have spoken over you may have made you feel unworthy. But God, the ultimate Father, has deemed you worthy and longs to see you step fully into your calling and operate in the specific gifts He has given to you.

Don't neglect the gifts, talents and abilities God has given you. Do not hold your gifts back from the Lord because He is the one who gave them to you. Allow God to do all that He has equipped and trained you to do in and through Him! The world needs your gifting. You will experience personal turnaround whenever you sink your life fully into whatever God has gifted you graced you to do.

CHAPTER 9

BREAKTHROUGH

I believe that God desires for each one of His sons and daughters to live and walk in His power. What does that look like? Well, God's power manifests in our lives in many different ways. However, often God's power is demonstrated in our lives by living a lifestyle of breakthrough. How can we talk about experiencing personal turnaround without talking about breakthrough?

When we are in need of a breakthrough it means that we are bound by something or have something keeping us from moving forward. We like to believe that our breakthrough will be a sudden boom or bang at the altar of one of those powerful conference gatherings.

I have personally had many breakthrough encounters at such altars. I have also had many breakthrough encounters in my private prayer times as well. There are numerous ways we can and will receive our breakthrough, but it often looks like enduring and contending until we see things change.

God spoke to me about breakthrough in a time of prayer and said, "Sometimes the breakthrough is simply the end of the process that God was using to take you toward a certain destination!" You must learn to endure and allow the process to teach and grow you. Crying and complaining about your situation will not change a single thing. In the process, before you get your breakthrough you must learn to be strong in your mind and to fully depend on God. Once you have a personal turnaround then you can release it to others! In the same way, if you want to help others receive their breakthrough you have to first get your own breakthrough!

If you do not break, you will have your breakthrough. God will use the hard times to prepare you. These times will be full of pressure, but you will come out properly equipped for your next season. Take courage; your breakthrough is at hand! The enemy will always try to wear you out and tire you out with a steady stream of intense warfare whenever he senses you are getting close to breakthrough. You must always remember to not look at where you are, but rather at where you are going. Never focus on the area in which you need breakthrough, but choose instead to hone in on the promises God has made to you. As you contend for breakthrough you must see each obstacle as a hurdle standing in your way to slow you down or distract you. Don't let the enemy or the distractions keep you from your breakthrough.

When I minister to people, I see breakthrough! Why? Because I have contended for breakthrough in my own life time and time again and came out victorious! When we experience breakthrough we begin to carry an anointing for breakthrough. What God does in our lives is never just about us. What God does in you, He will do through you. So fight for your breakthrough because many others' breakthroughs are on the other side. As breakthrough is released, our faith grows, our endurance is strengthened and we are able to step into the breathtaking things of the Lord. Expect your breakthrough!

Ephesians 6:10 says, "Now finally, my beloved ones, be supernaturally infused with strength through your life-union with the Lord Jesus. Stand victorious with the force of his explosive power flowing in and through you." God releases His explosive power to us so that we can understand the authority that has been given to us. Then we are supposed to let the power within us leak out into every single part of our lives and onto every person we come in contact with. You are anointed for breakthrough, don't settle for anything less.

The Apostle Paul understood the power of walking in the power of God and in breakthrough. Romans 15:29 says, "And I am sure that, when I come unto you, I shall come in the fullness of the blessing of Jesus Christ." Paul was completely convinced that when he visited a group of people that the gifts of the Spirit would be manifested. No matter what the people needed, Paul felt confident in his walk with God that if anyone needed breakthrough that the power of God would be present to minister to the people. Paul's life was one that was 100% completely devoted to God. Romans 1:11 says, "For I long to see you, that I may impart unto you some spiritual gifts, to the end you will be established." Paul had such a relationship with the Lord that when he went to minister, the impartation of the gifts of the Spirit of God would manifest themselves in the lives of the people that he ministered to. Paul knew they would receive these gifts and keep them until the end. We must understand that this delegated authority and power that God has given us is so real and necessary for today. To experience personal turnaround you need to walk in the power of God which releases breakthrough.

Luke 10:19 says, "Behold, I give you the authority to trample on serpents and scorpions, and over all the power of the enemy, and nothing shall by any means hurt you." If God has given you this authority what are you doing with it? Proverbs 18:21 tells us that "Death and life are in the power of the tongue." We discussed the power of declarations and decrees earlier in the book but your mouth can be your greatest weapon for breakthrough. Whenever you encounter a situation or a circumstance where there needs to be breakthrough begin to declare it out of your mouth. Many people do not experience breakthrough because they do not use the authority God has given them! Use your words as a weapon against the enemy and break through!

Many of you are believing for breakthrough in your life. You are believing for God to breakthrough in many different areas and bring change and transformation. When you sow breakthrough, you will reap breakthrough. As we seek the Kingdom of God first, then God takes care of everything else. In 2 Samuel 5:20, David is going up to battle. Scripture tells us that he went straight to Baal-Perazim and "He smashed his enemies to pieces. Afterwards, David said, "God has exploded my enemies like a gush of water. Then, David named that place, "the Master who explodes." Another translation says, "David named this place, "the Lord of the Breakthrough." Always remember that He is the God of the breakthrough in your life!

CHAPTER 10
🔥 MINDSET

I believe that if you can get your mindset right, there is nothing that can stop you from reaching your full potential in God. Like I have said before, I have seen so many people who have immense potential never accomplish anything. Why? All because of a wrong mindset. In this chapter, we will discuss the next key for personal turnaround which is having the right mindset.

Over the years of life and ministry, I have learned that in the first 3-5 minutes of speaking with someone I can get a good sense of the type of mindset they have. The way people speak and the words they use are good indicators of what their mindset is like. Unfortunately, if someone is negative, it is extremely obvious within the first few minutes of speaking with them. When I sense that someone may have a wrong or negative mindset, I don't set myself up to judge them. Instead, I think of ways I can help them to shift it.

Philippians 2:5 says, "Let this mind be in you which was also in Christ Jesus." This simply means that, as believers, we are to have the mind of Christ about everything in our lives. Whenever I encounter a hard, difficult or weird situation, I will pray this scripture. I pray to have the mind of Christ. I pray that I would see the situation or person the way God sees them. I pray that I would think about the situation the way the Lord does. I pray for my mindset and perspective to be like His. Why do I do this? Because I want to respond and make decisions in a Christ-like manner.

Philippians 4:8-9 says, "So keep your thoughts continually fixed on all that is authentic and real, honorable and admirable, beautiful and respectful, pure and holy, merciful and kind. And fasten your thoughts on every glorious work of God, praising Him always. Follow the example of all that we have imparted to you and the God of peace will be with you in all things." Each time you interact with someone, you can choose to find the good in them or the bad. In every situation, you can choose to see the positive or the negative. Our mindset is shaped by the choices we make about our thoughts and outlook on life. If we choose to always be negative, our mindset will continue to become more negative. However, if we choose to focus on those things that are admirable, good, just, and praise-worthy then our mindset will become more positive. Our mindset affects our choices and our choices affect our mindset. Kenneth Copeland says, "Those that think they can and those that think they can't are both right!" If your mindset tells you that you can do anything in life, then you will be able to do anything. If your mindset tells you that you can't do anything in life, then you won't. Your purpose and destiny can be derailed by the wrong mindset.

Proverbs 23:7 says, "For as a man thinks in his heart, so is he." In scripture, the word heart includes our spirit and our soul. We are three-part beings. We have a body, we are a spirit and we have a soul which is made up of our mind, our will and our emotions. So, Proverbs is saying here that whatever we think in our mind, emotions or spirit is what we will become. We must be stable in our emotions, strong in our spirit and have the right mindset in order to reach our destiny. This is why a shift in your mindset is a powerful key for personal turnaround.

1 Samuel 30:6 says, "Now David was greatly distressed, for the people spoke of stoning him, because the soul of all the people was grieved, every man for his sons and his daughters. But David encouraged himself in the Lord, his God." King David had every reason to be worried and distressed. Everyone around him wanted to kill him! But instead of giving in to his emotions or fear, David chose to strengthen himself by encouraging himself in the Lord. Each morning, I stand in front of the mirror, look myself in the eye and say, "Joe Joe Dawson, you are going to have a great day. You are going to have a powerful day. You are going to move forward in

every area of your life." I speak encouragement and life over myself every day. I do not look at my circumstances, difficult situations or what anyone else has said about me. I declare what God has said about me over myself. Each time you declare something, you are strengthening your mindset. This is true whether the declaration is positive or negative. If you declare that nothing good ever happens to you, this strengthens a negative mindset. But if you declare that God's goodness and favor chase you down, then your positive mindset will be strengthened.

My second daughter, Judah, is strong-minded and strong-willed. One summer, she created an exercise routine to stay in shape while she was out of school. She was explaining her routine to me and I was impressed with how rigorous it was. Part of her routine was to walk part of the time and run part of the time. So, she went outside and I went along to watch her. Summertime in Texas is no joke. It was already very hot outside that morning. After just a few minutes of running, her face was flushed and she was dripping with sweat but she just kept going. As Judah ran, she never once stopped to complain about how hot it was or how tired she was from running in the heat. After several more minutes, the Dad in me rose up and I stopped her and asked, "Judah, it's pretty hot out here. How much longer are you going to do this?" She replied, "Just 5 more minutes," and took off running again. Judah did not stop until the time she set for her exercise session was complete. Strong-minded people ignore their feelings and their flesh. Strong-minded people are determined to keep going even when it is difficult. They do not quit! You need a strong mind and a finishing spirit!

Every apple seed has a tree inside of it. Each seed has the potential to produce countless fruit. Your mindset must be to see the apples inside of the apple seed. When others see only apples, see the potential for orchards. Look at the people around you and call out their potential even when they are in seed form. John 12:24 says, "Most assuredly, I say to you, unless a grain of wheat falls into the ground and dies, it remains alone; but if it dies, it produces much grain." Some people stay in seed form, with untapped potential because they never die to their flesh and open up in order to produce fruit. The reason many people are unsuccessful is not because they are void of potential but because they haven't been willing to plant themselves in the will of God. To produce fruit and multiply ourselves we must be willing to die to the flesh.

Successful people think differently than the average person. I learned a valuable lesson from my dad when I was very young. When my dad was young, he worked in a factory line. At one point during his time working there, the management began letting many of the employees go. They were making budget cuts and laying people off. Instead of having the mindset of a victim or giving in to his circumstances, my dad had a different mindset. He told me, "Son, my goal at work is to outwork the person beside me. I am going to outwork the man on my right and my left. I am going to make myself valuable to this company by outworking everyone around me." Because of this mindset, my dad never lost his job. My dad instilled this work ethic into me and it has made a huge difference in my life. If you have an average mindset you will have an average work ethic. If you have an average work ethic, you will live an average life. Winners, champions and successful people do what others are unwilling to do.

People who are spiritually and emotionally strong react to things differently than those who are not. It is all about your mindset. Those who have spiritual and emotional stability are good stewards. Emotional and mental stability is so important. Your mindset can either lead you to success or to failure. Ask the Lord to prepare you and give you a strong mindset. Ask the Lord to establish you and make you stable in your mind and emotions. 1 Corinthians 2:16 assures us that we have the mind of Christ. Tap into that promise and allow the Lord to give you His mindset. If you have a turnaround in your thinking, you will experience a personal turnaround in many areas of your life.

CHAPTER 11
🔥 CHARACTER

There are so many key aspects to living a successful life and accomplishing the assignment God has given you. However, I believe that being a person of character and integrity is one of the most crucial. You cannot maintain anything that God entrusts to you, including personal turnaround, without character. Proverbs 22:1 says, "A good name is more desirable than great riches; to be esteemed is better than silver or gold." There are many people in the body of Christ who are incredibly gifted and talented with amazing abilities but they lack character. I am often asked, "Would you rather have someone who is highly gifted or someone with character?"

My answer is always the same, "Character!" I would, of course, prefer someone who is both gifted and has character but unfortunately, that is rare. John Maxwell says, "If you can be anything in this world, be someone people can count on."

As a leader, my main desire is to help people be successful in life. Whenever I meet people who are interested in becoming a part of our Apostolic Network or our church, they will often talk to me the most about their giftings or accomplishments. I warn each person interested in running with us that if they do not possess godly character, they will be unable to run with us for very long. We only run with people who are passionate about prayer, the presence and power of God and those that have good, strong character.

True character is who you are when no one else is around. Someone's true character will always be revealed. People will often see your gifts, talents, and abilities. However, you know you better than anyone. Are you a person of character? Character and integrity are so important because your gifts will get you to a certain level. However, it is your character that will keep you there. Poor character will remove you from any level you achieve because only good character can keep you there. Autumn and I have made a commitment to only promote those that we know have true character and integrity. We decided a long time ago that we would not let anyone destroy themselves on the platform God has given to us.

A leader's gift is only as safe as the character that surrounds it. You need to make sure you surround your God-given gifts, talents, and abilities with character. When I was a kid, I would always go out with my grandfather and help him plant tomatoes. We would till up the soil and plant the tomato seeds. Then, my grandfather would always put thin metal wire cages around the tomato plants. I remember one year asking him why he put the cages around the seeds. My grandfather explained to me that the metal wire was to keep animals and pests out of the plant so that it could grow healthy and grow lots of tomatoes. Character in your life is like those metal wire cages. Character will protect the fruit of your life.

Proverbs 11:3 says, "The integrity of the upright will guide them, but the perversity of the unfaithful will destroy them." I do not want to be a flash in the pan in ministry, business, marriage, parenting or any area of my life. I want to be faithful and have integrity in everything that I do because I want to leave a powerful legacy for my biological and spiritual children. John Maxwell says, "It's true that charisma can make a person stand out for a moment, but character sets a person apart for a lifetime." Your character determines your length of stay in a lot of places. In my many years of ministry, I have seen the same situation play out over and over again. A couple, a family or an individual will come into a church and become very involved in either serving or leadership. Then, the first time there is a character flaw that is addressed by the leadership, they will leave. I've seen so many people leave ministries and businesses because they do not want to deal with their character flaws. Instead of changing and growing, they go from church to church or workplace to workplace and never become a person of character.

Leaders are held to a higher standard. Dr. Myles Munroe said, "We lead out of our beliefs." A person who is full of character changes the room when he or she walks in. People who have high standards will convict those around them just with their lifestyle. If you lead a ministry, business or organization, the people will start to adopt your level of character and integrity. They will follow the example you set. In today's society, people rarely forgive those in the public eye if they have some sort of public failure. Society holds past failures over people. Make it really hard for people to find any dirt on you. Live a life of such integrity that if someone wants to slander you or talk bad about you, they have to make up lies to do so. 1 Peter 3:16 says, "With gentleness and respect maintain a clean conscience so that those who slander you for living a pure life in Christ will have to lie about you and will be ashamed because of their slander." When critics say things about you, you never have to respond in self-defense. Your character will do the talking.

Proverbs 10:9 says, "Whoever walks in integrity walks securely, but whoever takes crooked paths will be found out." People who lack good character will always be found out. Likewise, those who have good character will be elevated by the Lord to places of great leadership and influence. Dr. Myles Munroe said, "Character is the foundation for all aspects of effective leadership." If you do not have character, your time in leadership will be cut short. The devil isn't in a hurry to get you. He will wait until you have influence. The more influence you have, the more the enemy will try to trap you. This is why you must work on your character every day. As God elevates you and increases your gifting, you must raise your standards and your level of integrity. Character is something that takes years to build but can be destroyed in a second! Don't let the enemy trap you by tempting you with the things of this world. Become a person of ever-increasing character and integrity.

You win the battles of life in the private place in the preparation season, not when the attacks actually come. Your beliefs are your personal standards and convictions in life. We must all stand for something in life! Our beliefs, standards, and convictions are birthed in the place of private prayer. Remember the power of prayer we talked about in Chapter 1! Leonard Ravenhill said, "A man who is not praying is straying." If you do not want to go astray, let God build your character in the secret place.

CHAPTER 12 ◑ THE WORD OF GOD

The next key for personal turnaround is the Word of God. The Word of God is so powerful. When we spend time in it daily, we will see transformation in ourselves and in every area of our lives.

I love the Bible! I love spending time reading and studying the Word of God. One of the reasons the Word of God is a key for personal turnaround is because the Word of God is life-giving to our entire being. The Word of God breathes life into our spirit, ministers to our soul and crucifies our flesh. Hebrews 4:12 says, "For we have the living Word of God, which is full of energy, and it pierces more sharply than a two-edged sword.

It will even penetrate to the very core of our being where soul and spirit, bone and marrow meet! It interprets and reveals the true thoughts and secret motives of our hearts." The Word cuts through all the things of the flesh.

This is one of my favorite passages of scripture and has been something I have based my life on for many years. Psalms 119:9-11 says, "How can a young man cleanse his way? By taking heed according to Your word. With my whole heart I have sought You. Oh, let me not wander from Your commandments! Your word I have hidden in my heart, that I might not sin against You." Whenever I see people in our ministry or people we minister to start to backslide or just look heavy, I always ask them this, "When did you stop reading the Word of God and spending time in prayer?" They are always shocked that I know they have stopped spending time reading and praying! However, it is so obvious to me when someone seems to be backsliding or has a poor countenance that they are not spending time in the Word of God. Why? Because the Word of God keeps us on track. It reveals what is soulish and what is from God's Spirit. It speaks truth into our lives and changes us from the inside out.

When you read the Word of God, it should come alive to you. Spending time reading the Bible will awaken dead dreams inside of you and bring life-giving energy to you. 2 Timothy 3:16-17 says, "Every scripture has been written by the Holy Spirit, the breath of God. It will empower you by its instruction and correction, giving you the strength to take the right direction and lead you deeper into the path of godliness. Then you will be God's servant, fully mature and perfectly prepared to fulfill any assignment God gives you." God's Word equips us for our purpose. Staying in the Word will keep you from turning to the right or to the left as you run after your destiny with God. Without the Word in our lives, we cannot be successful.

John 1:1 says, "In the beginning was the Word, and the Word was with God, and the Word was God." God gave us His Word because Jesus is the Word of God! When you read the Word of

God on a daily basis and spend time praying and meditating on it, there is no way you can fail in life. Psalms 119:105 says, "Your word is a lamp to my feet and a light to my path." The more we read the Word of God, the hungrier we will be for it. If you ask God to give you a desire for His Word, He will give it to you! When we are hungry for the Word of God, we will spend every free moment reading and studying it. I remember when I was in my 20's. I worked helping my father with his cattle business. I would carry my small Gideon's Bible in my back pocket with me to work each day. Every time I had a free moment, I would pull it out and read it. When I had just started fully walking with the Lord, I developed a passion and a hunger for the Word of God that is still with me today. All the days of my life I want to be a student of the Bible. If we will stay forever a learner, Jesus will be our forever teacher. There is always more of God and I want to always be hungry for more of Him.

In John 17:17, Jesus is praying for His disciples and He prays this, "Sanctify them by Your truth. Your Word is truth." I have seen many people get off of the Word of God and be led astray. Any time you get a prophetic word, no matter who it is from, you need to make sure it lines up with the written Word of God. I love the prophetic! I decree and declare the prophetic promises God has given me all the time. However, we must make sure that any prophetic word we receive is in agreement with the Bible. Don't let any false prophecies get you off track or deceive you. The Word of God is 100% truth and we need to use it as the standard we measure all other words by.

In Matthew 7:27 Jesus says this, "Therefore whoever hears these sayings of Mine, and does them, I will liken him to a wise man who built his house on the rock." This scripture is stating that the Word of God is supposed to be the foundation we build our entire life upon. When the Word is our foundation, it doesn't matter what kind of attacks the enemy throws at us or what circumstances, trials and tests we may go through. We will stand! One time at a conference I was attending, one of the speakers shared this simple illustration. He took his Bible, laid it on the ground and stood on it. He said,

"When I stand upon the Word of God, I stand just a little bit taller. When we make the Word our foundation, we will not be moved."

There are over 7,000 promises found in the Bible. You need to have scriptures that you stand upon. I quote the Word of God over myself, my family, our ministry and our business every single day. Matthew 4:4 says, "But He (Jesus) answered and said, "It is written, 'Man shall not live by bread alone, but by every word that proceeds from the mouth of God.'" When we quote the Word of God it brings power to our life. When we declare the Word of God over our lives and our loved ones there is nothing that can destroy us. In Luke 11:28 Jesus says, "More than that, blessed are those who hear the word of God and keep it!" The Bible says that God watches over His Word to perform it. This is why saturating our lives with scripture is so important. Whenever I hear a scripture and it goes off in my spirit, I will go and study that scripture out. Each time I hear someone preach a message there are always one or two scriptures that stand out to me and I will write them down and then spend time reading them and digging deep into them. Dig deep into the Word of God every chance that you get! Set aside time every day to read scripture and you will see your whole life transformed. The Word of God is a powerful tool to see personal turnaround in your life. Allow the Lord to make you hungry for His Word and declare it over your life!

CHAPTER 13
⊙ HEALTH

In the first 12 chapters, I've talked to you about the spirit and the soul. We've discussed the many different ways you can personally turn your life around to be more effective for God. When you apply the first 12 things I've talked about so far, you will be able to manifest the Kingdom of God and use the gifts God has placed inside of you.

1 Thessalonians 5:23 says, "May God Himself, the God of peace sanctify you through and through, may your whole spirit, soul and body be kept blameless at the coming of our Lord Jesus Christ." So, I now want to talk to you about the body. I want to share with you my personal turnaround in my health that transformed my life.

In the middle of 2019, I was sitting on my back porch watching my daughters play the sport they love, volleyball. In fact, our whole family loves it, however, I was unable to join in on the family fun. Just before this, I had gone through a double hernia surgery. After the surgery, I did not fully recover like I thought I would. I had been crying out to God, asking for a personal turnaround physically. I knew that if I lost weight it would take some pressure off of the incisions from the double hernia and the areas where they inserted the medical mesh. Working out wasn't an option for me due to the fact that I was recovering from surgery, so I was looking for an answer through nutrition to help me lose a few pounds. A few days later, I got in contact with one of my mentors in life who is a Certified Health Coach with a company called Optavia. I asked him if I got on the program, would I be able to lose 10 or 12 pounds in a few weeks. My Health Coach told me that I could easily lose 20 or more pounds on the program.

I started the program and in three days I got into a fat burn, and I felt great for the first time in months. My wife noticed that I had gained so much energy and mental clarity that she decided to join me on this journey towards health. I ended up losing 19 pounds in the first two weeks of the program. Our friends and family members began to ask us questions about our transformation so my wife and I decided to pay it forward and we became certified health coaches in order to help others.

A few years ago, I weighed 255 pounds, and today, as I'm writing this, I weigh 187. When I started Optavia I lost a lot of weight. The weight I lost took the pressure off of my midsection where the medical mesh had been inserted and I gained so much energy by fueling my body properly. Now, I feel more effective in my physical body to be able to carry out the purpose, dreams, and destiny that God has called me to. My wife and I, in just a few short months, lost a total of 70 pounds. It has been so exciting to walk with others on their journey as they receive freedom in their physical bodies from obesity, disease, and sickness. When you take your health back, you will have a personal turnaround physically and it will clear the fog from your mind.

Each of us has a race that has been set before us, and we don't want to wear out our bodies before we cross the finish line. We want to finish strong! I want to encourage you today, take your health back! Have a personal turnaround in your body, begin to do some healthy movement daily like exercising, working out, or walking. Begin to drink more water, it's so good for you. Start saying yes to lean healthy proteins and vegetables and no to the empty calories that you are just casually putting in your body. This is important because what God has called us to do in the near future will require us to be ready! We must be ready not only in our spirit and soul but also in our bodies. What God is about to do in the New Era and in the body of Christ we must all be prepared to go 100%, all in, full-throttle after the things of God. 3 John 1:2 declares, "Beloved, I pray that in every way you may prosper and be in good health, just as your soul prospers."

CONCLUSION

I hope that these keys for personal turnaround have revolutionized the way you think! If you will implement these 13 keys in your life, there is no way you can fail. As you live a life of prayer and fasting, sow into the Kingdom of God, war with your prophetic promises and surround yourself with powerful mentors, you will become everything God has called you to be.

God has a breathtaking purpose and destiny for your life. You will watch me do everything that God has called me to do. But will I get to watch you do everything He has called you to do? I want to challenge you to get your personal turnaround and run hard after the things of God.

It does not matter what your life or circumstances may look like right now, God can turn it all around. Nothing is impossible with God! There is no limit to what you can do if you will seek the Kingdom of God first in your life. Don't look back at your past experiences or failures any longer. Put the past behind you and live a life full of purpose and destiny. Personal turnaround is possible and I hope this has helped you to move forward into your God-given destiny. God is going to use you to bring turnaround in your city, region, nation and in the earth so go for it, my friends! This is your season for personal turnaround!

ABOUT THE AUTHOR

Joe Joe Dawson is the Founder and Apostle of Roar Apostolic Network and Roar Church Texarkana. Joe Joe is married to the love of his life, Autumn Dawson. Together they have three children Malachi, Judah, and Ezra. The Dawson's teach a lifestyle of revival and awakening. Their desire is to see every believer fulfill their God-given destiny and live life to the fullest in God. Joe Joe is the author of The 40 P's Of The Apostolic, Destiny Dimensions, and Living Your God-Sized Dream. He is also the host of Kingdom Mindset Podcast on the Charisma Podcast Network.

CONNECT WITH JOE JOE

JOE JOE DAWSON
FACEBOOK

@JOE_JOE_DAWSONTXK
INSTAGRAM

@PASTORJOEDAWSON
TWITTER

JOE JOE DAWSON
YOUTUBE

@JOEJOEDAWSON
PERISCOPE

JOEJOEDAWSON.NET
WEBSITE

The Kingdom Mindset podcast encourages, equips, trains, and motivates listeners to fulfill their purpose and destiny with a Kingdom mindset. Join host Joe Joe Dawson as he explores and dives into a wide range of topics that will transform and inspire you to become all that God has called you to be. Tune in every Monday at CharismaPodcastNetwork.com

Roar Apostolic Network is a network of believers who are contending for revival and awakening. Our heart is to help train and equip every person and ministry that comes into alignment with us. We are called to walk in the fullness of God's authority and power while abiding in the Father's love. Our calling is to help others reach their God-given dreams and destiny. This network is built for a church, ministry, pastor, business person, intercessor, believer, etc. ROAR stands for Revival, Outpouring, Awakening, and Reformation.

For more information, visit roarapostolicnetwork.com

WEBSITES · BOOK DESIGN · GRAPHICS
MCFARLAND-CREATIVE.COM

All of Joe Joe Dawson's books have been administrated by McFarland Creative. McFarland Creative offers full book facilitation that includes book editing, interior design, formatting & cover design. We will take your vision for the book inside of you and make it a reality. If you are interested in sharing your words with the world, email info@mcfarland-creative.com today!

9 781735 080000